LIFE AMONG THE DEAD IN THE TRENCHES

HISTORY WAR BOOKS
CHILDREN'S MILITARY BOOKS

Speedy Publishing LLC

40 E. Main St. #1156

Newark, DE 19711

www.speedypublishing.com

Copyright 2017

In this book, we're going to talk about the conditions of soldiers who fought in the trenches in World War I. So, let's get right to it!

WORLD WAR SOLDIERS FIRING
FROM A TRENCH

World War I was primarily fought in the trenches. The pattern of the fighting and the daily life of the soldiers varied a great deal depending on the location. More than likely most soldiers who signed up to fight had no idea how little ground they would cover during the war. Trench warfare was very slow and the conditions were very unsanitary and hazardous.

A WAR WITH LITTLE MOVEMENT

Most countries didn't expect World War I, also called the Great War, to last very long. They expected the action to be quick moving and to cover a tremendous amount of ground. However, for the ground troops, the exact opposite was true. For the years from 1914 until 1918, the trench warfare meant that the movement forward was very slow.

WW1 TRENCH WARFARE

WESTERN FRONT

The war began with the dramatic advances by the German armies through the country of Belgium and the country of France on their way to the city of Paris. However, as soon as trench warfare began, the movement slowed to a crawl. The line on the Western Front did change as local battles were won and lost, but in general there was not much movement until the war was almost over.

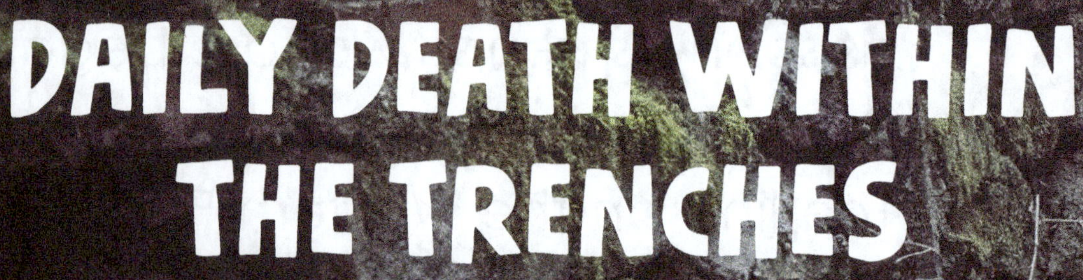

DAILY DEATH WITHIN THE TRENCHES

Death was a daily occurrence in the trenches. Even if no active battle was taking place, disease took its toll. In areas where active battles were ongoing, the endless firing of shells brought a quick and random death.

FIRST WORLD WAR TRENCHES

DUGOUTS

There were dugout shelters in the trenches and heavy fire would sometimes cause a collapse and bury the men alive.

SNIPERS

New soldiers were told not to look out over the top of the trench into the area between their trench and the enemy's. This stretch of land was called "No Man's Land" and many a curious soldier peered over only to be quickly hit by an enemy sniper bullet.

It's been estimated that over one third of the men who died fighting for the Allied Powers died in the trenches. Many men were killed the very first day they fought.

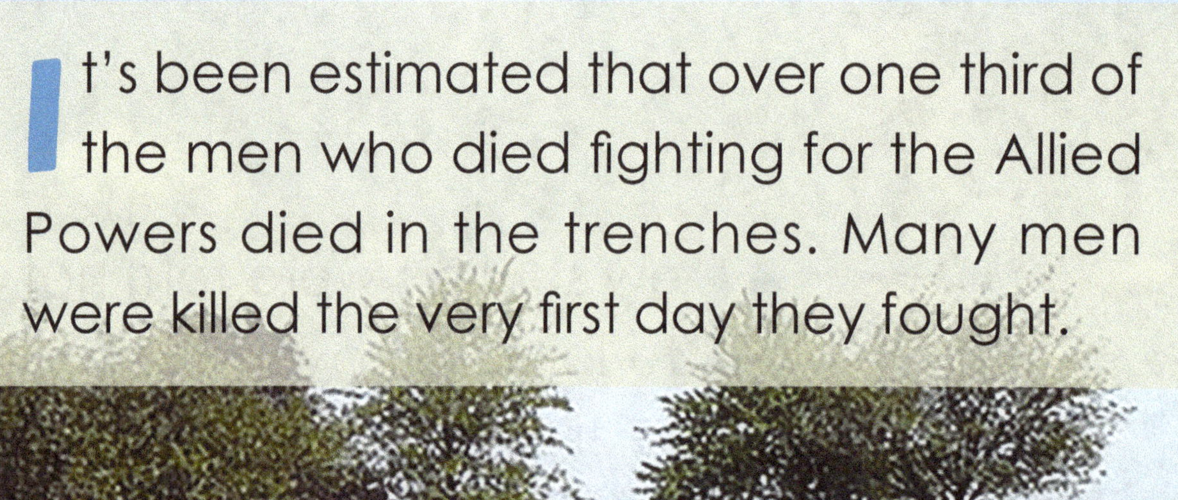

WW1 CEMETERY

owever, a sniper's bullet wasn't the only danger. Due to the unsanitary conditions, disease claimed many soldiers as well.

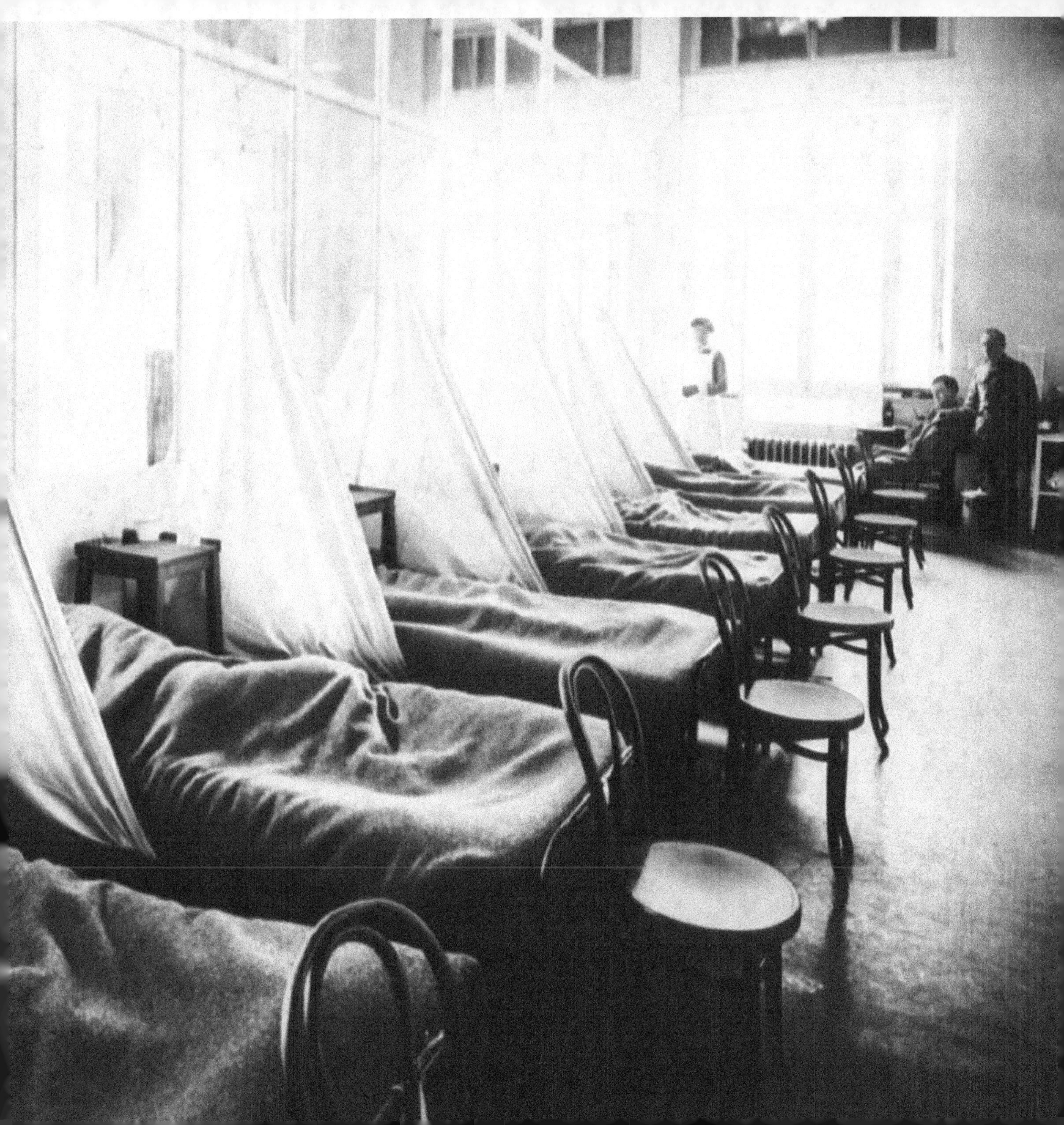

INFESTATION OF RATS

There were millions of rats in the trenches with the men. Black rats were hated, but the brown rats were feared as well as hated. This is because the brown rats would go after remains of the dead soldiers. They would disfigure the corpses by eating their eyes and their livers. There was a lot for the rats to eat and sometimes they grew as large as cats.

At night, when the men tried to sleep, rats would run over their faces as an ever-present reminder of what would happen to their bodies if they died in the trenches. The soldiers would shoot the rats, or club them, or stab them with bayonets, but it was a hopeless exercise.

BAYONET KNIVES

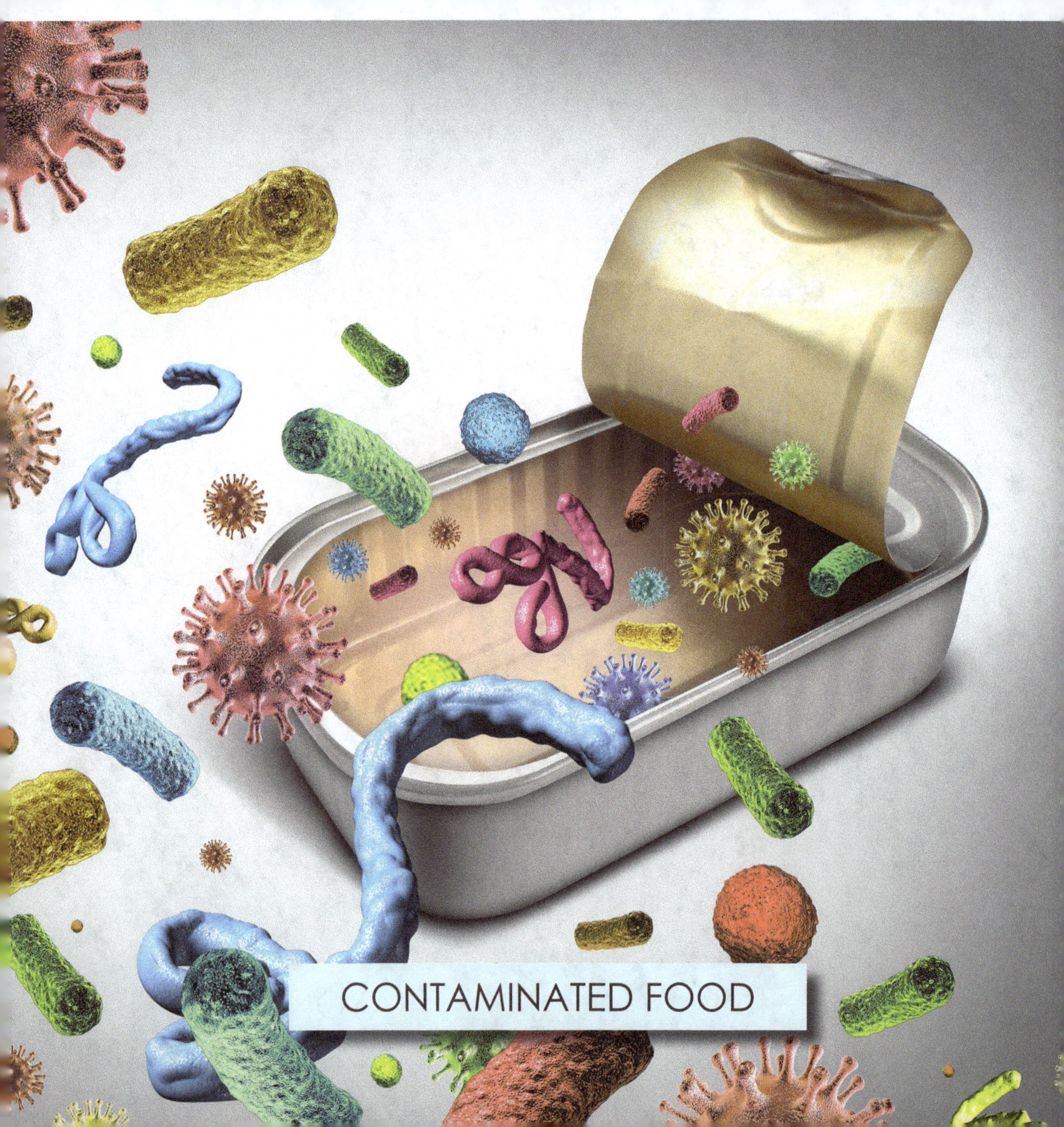
CONTAMINATED FOOD

Just one pair of rats was able to give birth to 900 more rats within a year. The rats continued to grow in numbers as they spread diseases and contaminated the supply of food.

AMERICAN SOLDIERS FIRING A
FRENCH 37 MM ARTILLERY GUN

When the rats decreased in numbers, it was frequently taken as a sign that the soldiers would soon come under very heavy enemy fire. Legend has it that the soldiers thought the rats could sense the coming blood bath and left so they and their offspring wouldn't be killed.

FROGS, LICE, NITS, SLUGS, AND BEETLES

As if the rats weren't bad enough, there were a host of other creatures in the trenches as well. Lice were everywhere. The men had filthy clothing and the lice multiplied within the clothing seams. The huge numbers of lice would cause the men to want to scratch their skin off.

HEAD LICE (LOUSE)

YOUNG MAN WITH RAZOR
SHAVING HEAD

Even when their uniforms were washed as well as deloused, the lice eggs, called nits, would stay hidden deep within the clothing seams. As soon as they put their washed clothes back on, their own body heat would cause the nits to hatch and more new lice would attack their skin. Many men shaved their heads completely just so they would not be overrun by nits.

No one realized this at the time, but the lice were also carrying a disease that was eventually called "Trench Fever." It was a very painful disease. It started suddenly when a soldier was wracked with intense pain and then very high fever. Such a solder was in no condition to fight and had to recover away from the trenches for 3 to 4 months or more. It wasn't discovered that lice had been the culprits in causing this disease until almost the end of the war.

VERY ILL MAN WITH WARM WATER
BOTTLE AND THERMOMETER

BIG BROWN FROG SITTING IN DITCH

Frogs were reproducing in the water at the bottom of the trenches. All types of slugs and large horned beetles crawled up the sides.

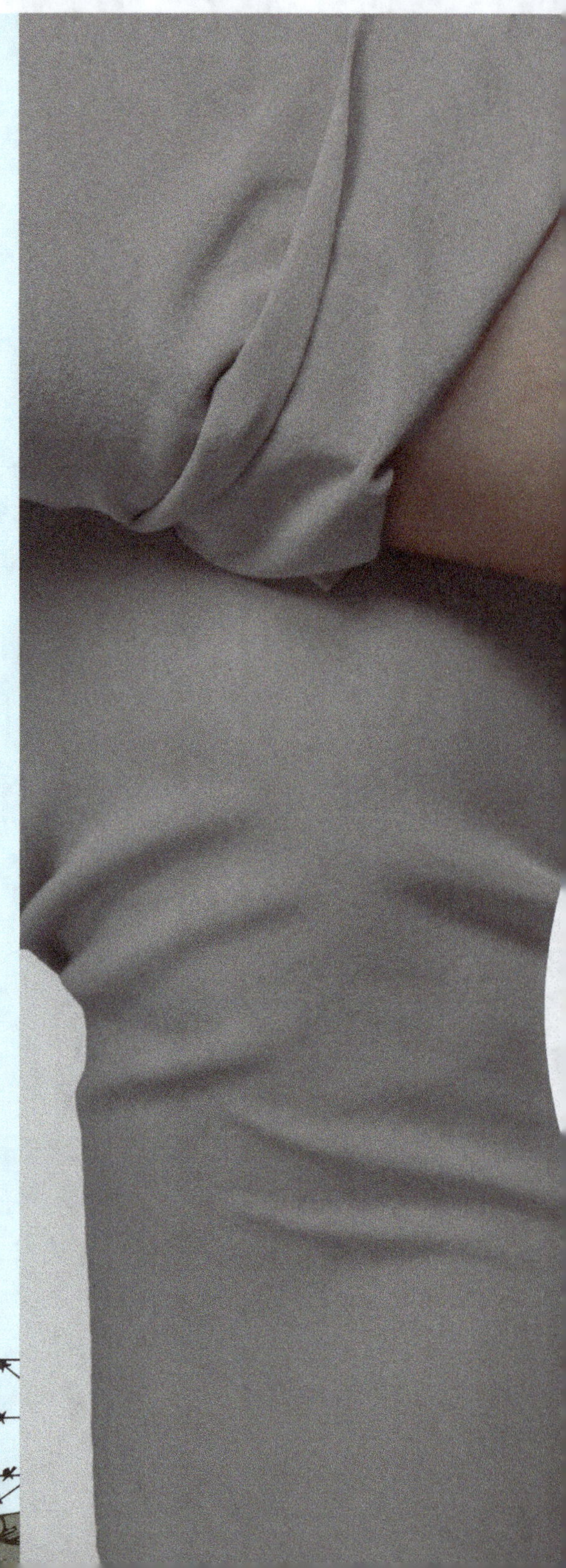

Another medical condition that caused pain and agony for the soldiers was a fungal infection called "Trench Foot." Their feet were almost always standing in water or mud that was very unsanitary causing their feet to become infected with a fungus.

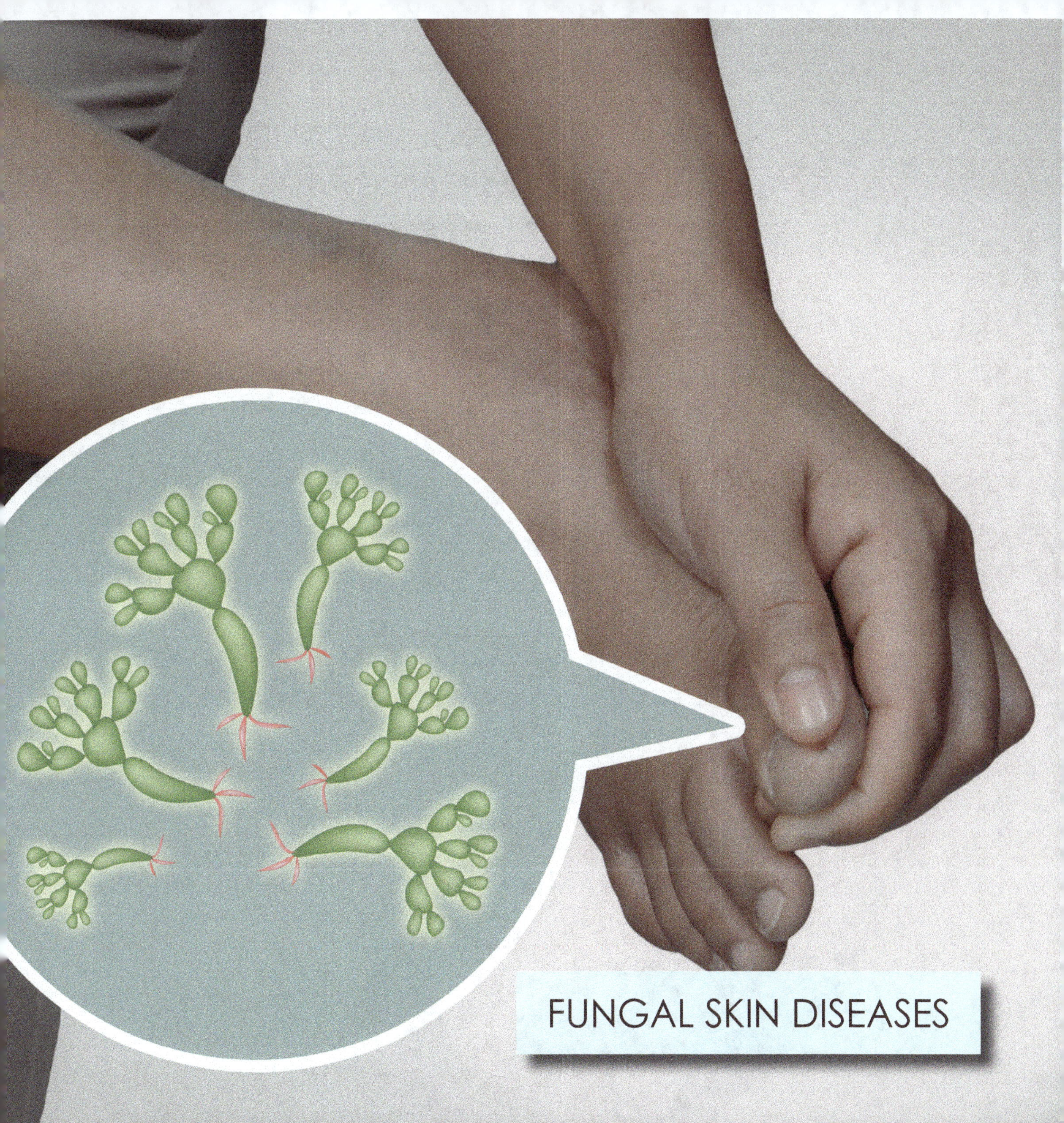

FUNGAL SKIN DISEASES

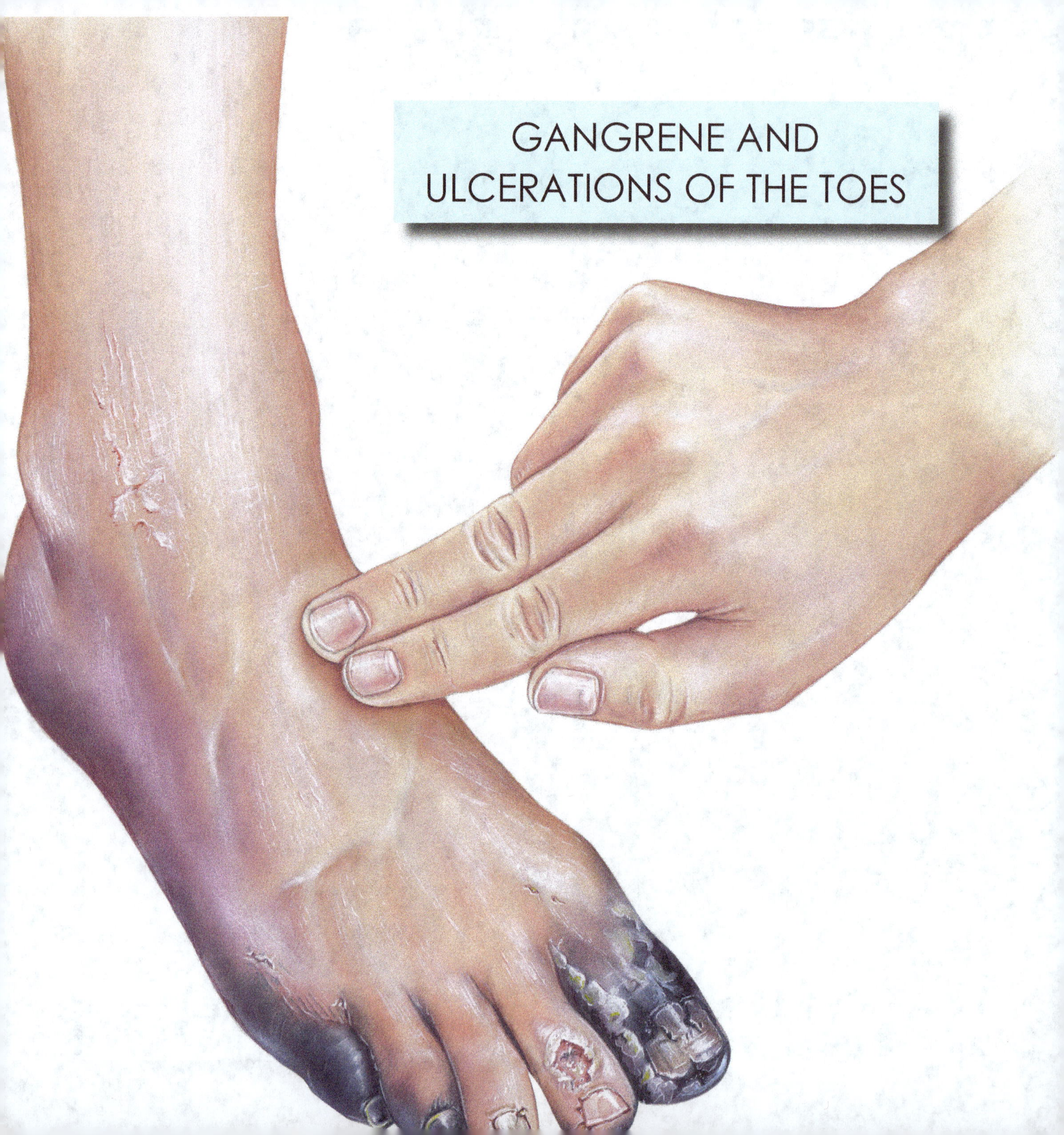

GANGRENE AND
ULCERATIONS OF THE TOES

If this infection wasn't treated and allowed to linger, it would turn to gangrene, which was the death of their tissues. The resulting black tissue couldn't be healed. This meant that the soldier would die unless his foot or part of his leg was amputated. By 1915, conditions improved and there were less cases of Trench Foot.

THE SMELL OF THE TRENCHES

Dead bodies were all around the trenches. On the Somme battlefield, over 200,000 men died and their bodies were thrown into shallow graves. The smell of rotting corpses and the latrines, which were overflowing, gave off an absolutely horrendous odor. Chloride of lime with a heavy bleach smell was used in the trenches to fight off disease from the unsanitary conditions.

A GLASS BOTTLE OF POISON
WITH TOXIC VAPOR

All this in combination with the smell of bodies that hadn't bathed in weeks, the leftovers of poison gas, and leftover smoke created a smell that made visitors to the trenches gag. The soldiers somehow got used to the hellish conditions.

THE TRENCH CYCLE

A battalion of soldiers would have a cycle of fighting and rest as they fought in the trenches. They would serve at the front lines and then they would serve as support for the front lines. After that, they would be in the back-up reserve lines for a time.

SOLDIERS MARCHING

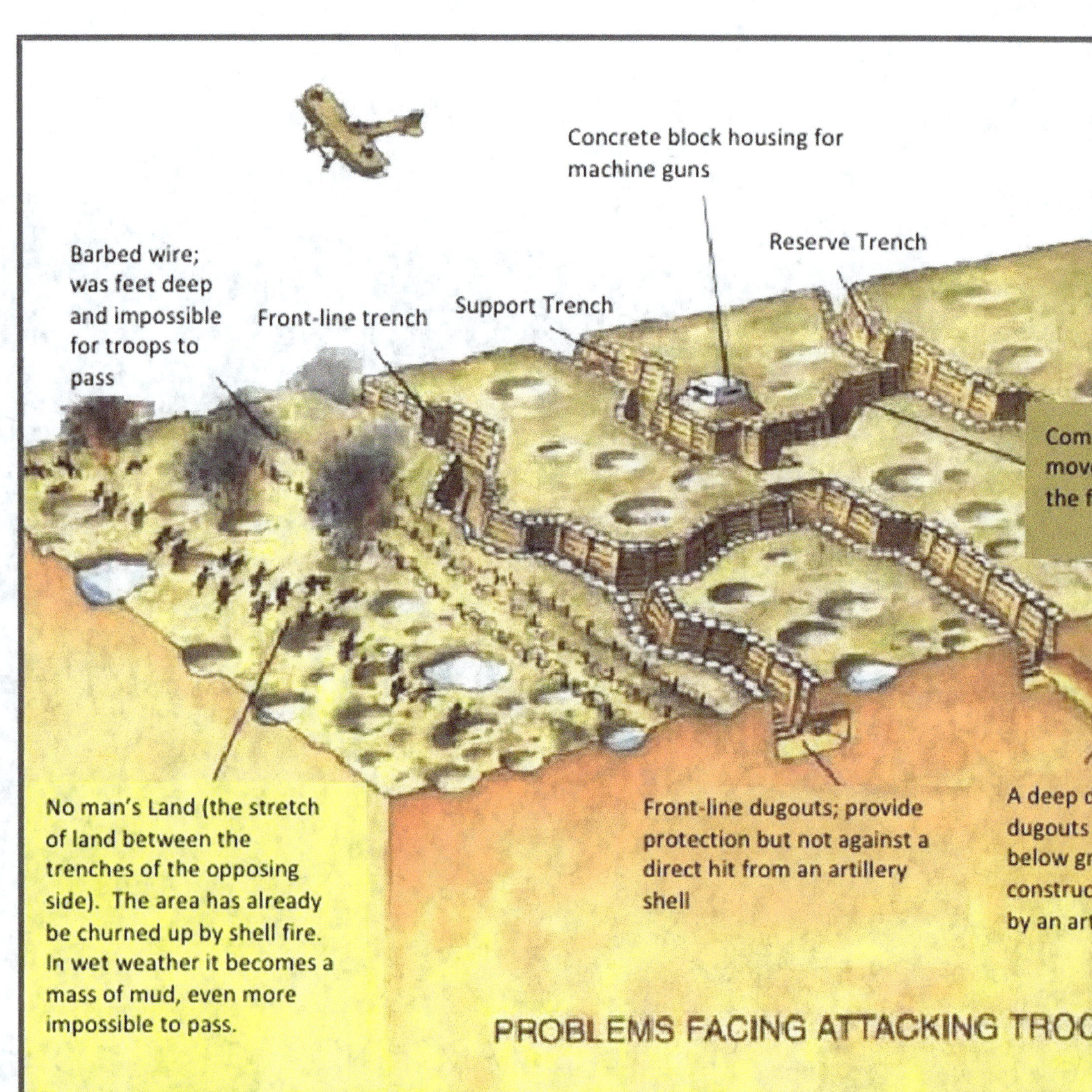

Concrete block housing for machine guns
Reserve Trench
Support Trench
Front-line trench
Barbed wire; was feet deep and impossible for troops to pass
Comr move the fr
No man's Land (the stretch of land between the trenches of the opposing side). The area has already be churned up by shell fire. In wet weather it becomes a mass of mud, even more impossible to pass.
Front-line dugouts; provide protection but not against a direct hit from an artillery shell
A deep d dugouts below gr construct by an art
PROBLEMS FACING ATTACKING TROO

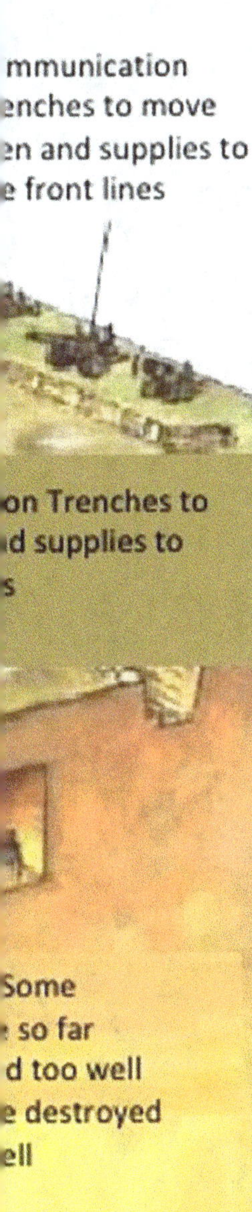

he support line trench was located behind the front line trench and the reserve line trench was located behind the support lines. Finally, the soldiers would have a short period of rest. Then, it was back to the front line again for a new cycle of duty in the trenches.

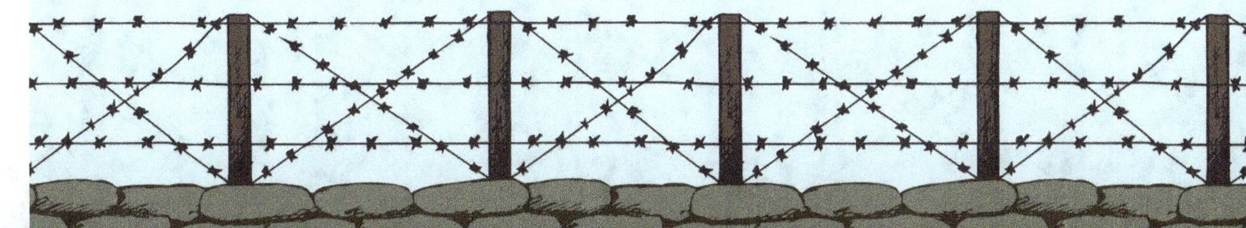

The number of days in each part of the cycle varied widely depending on the status at the front lines. Within a year, a particular soldier might spend about 70 days at the very front line and another 30 days in the support lines. Another 120 days would be spent in the very back in the reserve lines. Another 70 days were designated for rest with only two weeks of leave during the entire year.

FRONTLINE TRENCH

STAND TO AND MORNING HATE

Every day there was a procedure and process that the men followed. They prepared an hour before the break of dawn. The head officer and the sergeant would wake the men up. They were made to climb up on the fire step so if the enemy tried to attack them as soon as there was light from the sun, they would be ready with their bayonets.

The fire-step ran along the length of the entire trench allowing the men to peer over the side through the parapet into "No Man's Land." This policy of being ready on the fire step was called "stand to" and both sides followed a similar procedure. Despite this readiness, many raids took place at dawn. This process of waiting for the light and waiting to be fired upon by the enemy was called "the morning hate."

THE MORNING HATE

GERMAN WW1 MACHINE GUN CREW
FIRING FROM A TRENCH

The early hours before "the morning hate" were very tense as the men prepared for another day of fighting. Sometimes they would relieve their tensions by firing machine guns or shelling in the direction of the enemy even though there wasn't enough sunlight to penetrate the mist. They couldn't see what they were shooting at.

After "the morning hate," breakfast would be brought by wagons. During this time period both sides sometimes maintained a truce although it wasn't official. When breakfast was over, there was inspection and then the men took care of the chores they were assigned. They would sometimes have to repair the trenches after periods of heavy rainfall.

WAGON HORSE

The "stand to" process was repeated at nightfall to guard against surprise attacks by the enemy as the sunlight faded away. As soon as it was dark, the men would handle supply and maintenance duties. The soldiers were expected to rotate at sentry duty. They each did this for about two hours. Any longer and they might fall asleep at their posts. The penalty for being caught sleeping was to be shot by a firing squad.

Now you know more about the fighting that took place in the trenches during World War I and the horrible conditions the soldiers endured. You can find more Military books from Baby Professor by searching the website of your favorite book retailer.

Visit
BABY PROFESSOR
EDUCATION KIDS
www.BabyProfessorBooks.com
to download Free Baby Professor eBooks
and view our catalog of new and exciting
Children's Books